TYNESIDE FROM THE AIR

TYNESIDE FROM THE AIR

WEBBAVIATION.CO.UK

breedon **books**
PUBLISHING

First published in Great Britain in 2009 by

The Breedon Books Publishing Company Limited

Breedon House, 3 The Parker Centre,

Derby, DE21 4SZ.

ISBN 978-1-85983-683-5

Printed and bound in China by 1010 Printing International Ltd.

Acknowledgements

There are a number of people who have helped in the making of this book and I would like to express particular thanks to John Seville, the UK's best aerial photographic pilot, whose skill at flying 'photobatics' is legendary and who flew me for most of the images in this book. I would also like to thank fellow aerial photographers William Cross and Catherine Wheildon for their constant support, my long-suffering partner Birgit Engsfeld, and Ian Hay of Flight Images who got me out of a hole: while I was flying over South Shields I got so excited by the departing cruise liner I missed out Arbeia Roman Fort for which Ian kindly provided the image.

Contents

With so many historical buildings and so much influential architecture, *Tyneside from the air* has been a joy to work on. I have tried to capture some of the vibrancy of the area and record it at a moment in time when it is undergoing great change. I have included the subjects you will expect, such as the Tynemouth priory, the River Tyne, the great shipyards and Antony Gormley's iconic sculpture, the Angel of the North. I hope I have also added a few surprises, such as my images of the Newcastle Green Festival, which show not just an area but the local people themselves.

The images have been a technical challenge and most were taken on a Canon 1Ds MkIII camera with a gyro-stabilised mount specially developed for aerial photography. This has enabled probably the highest resolution civilian aerial photographs of Tyneside ever taken from a moving aeroplane.

I hope you enjoy reading this book as much as I have enjoyed taking the photographs.

Newcastle

Previous page: Newcastle upon Tyne city centre looking south, with Gateshead in the background.

This page: 55 Degrees North
Built as an office block and previously known as Swan House, the building was a bold design straddling the roundabout. Recently the building has been renovated and now provides mixed residential and commercial space, including the Metro Radio offices. The renovation included the design of a new public space and reworking of pedestrian access, which involved the shortening of the subway on the left and replacing one subway with a ground level pedestrian crossing, seen in the bottom centre of the image. The most striking feature of the refurbishment is the pink wall designed to screen the clutter of structures behind. The redevelopment has been awarded the Lord Mayor's design award for urban landscape.

Holy Jesus Hospital Almshouse

Although most of what we see today dates from the 17th century, parts of the building date back to the 14th-century Augustinian Friary that previously occupied the site and was dissolved in 1539. The tower was probably constructed in around the 16th century as an armoury and strong point. The Holy Jesus Hospital was built in 1681 as a home for retired freemen and their families. Although the hospital moved out in 1937, the building has been preserved and protected from the redevelopment of the area which took place in the 1960s and saw many of the other older buildings demolished. The building is owned by Newcastle City Council and run on their behalf by the National Trust.

Above: Tyne Bridge and the *Tuxedo Princess*

Opened in 1928 by King George V, the Tyne Bridge was designed by Mott Hay and Anderson, who also designed the Forth Bridge. The *Tuxedo Princess*, shown here shortly before she was moved to Greece in 2008, was built in 1961 for the Caledonian Steam Ship company and named the *Caledonian Princess*. After finishing service as a ferry in 1981, she was converted to a nightclub famous for her revolving dance floor.

Left: All Saints' Church was constructed in 1796 to a distinctive elliptical design by David Stephenson, replacing the previous mediaeval church. Religious use ceased in 1961 and the building is now used as an office and auditorium.

The Swing Bridge and High Level Bridge

The Swing Bridge was designed and built by Sir William Armstrong and opened in 1876. It is on the site of the original Roman bridge built in the second century AD by Emperor Hadrian. The Roman Bridge lasted until 1248 when it, along with much of the town, was destroyed in a great fire. A second bridge was built in 1320, which lasted until it was destroyed in a flood in 1771. The third bridge on the site was built in 1781, but was replaced by the swing bridge to allow larger ships to navigate further up the River Tyne.

Opened in 1849 by Queen Victoria, the High Level Bridge was designed by Robert Stephenson and carries road traffic on its lower deck with the railway, being on the upper deck. The bridge was restored between 2006 and 2008 and now vehicular access is limited to public transport going south.

The King Edward VII Bridge
Designed by Charles A. Harrison, the King Edward VII Bridge was opened by its namesake on 10 July 1906.

Above: The Byker Estate

Right: The Byker Wall. Designed by Ralph Erskine to replace run-down Victorian terraces, the Wall has won many awards, including the Civic Trust Award, the Ambrose Congreve Award for housing, the Eternit Award and the Veronica Rudge Green Prize for urban design from Harvard University. The Wall is on UNESCO's list of outstanding 20th-century buildings and in 2007 was granted a Grade II listing.

Previous Page: Newcastle and its bridges. From the foreground, the Redreugh Bridge, King Edward VII Bridge, the Queen Elizabeth II Metro Bridge (in blue), the High Level Bridge, Tyne Bridge and finally the Millennium Bridge.

Newcastle University

The university's origins date back to the School of Medicine and Surgery opened in 1834 and the Armstrong College founded in 1871. The two merged in 1937 to form the Kings College and became the University of Newcastle upon Tyne in 1963.

The university has over 2,000 members of teaching staff and more than 18,000 students, including overseas students from more than 100 countries, and it won *The Sunday Times* University of the Year award in 2000. There is a strong emphasis on research, especially in medical sciences, with current projects including a vaccine for arthritis, research into the ageing process and stem cell research.

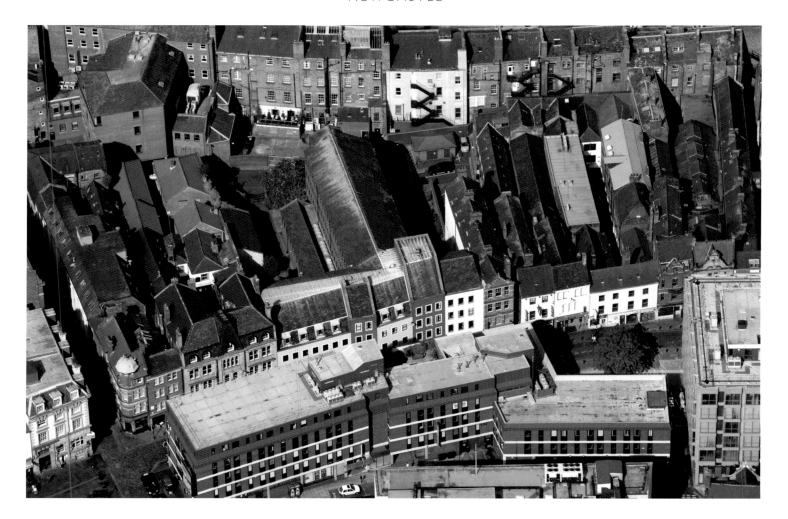

The Cloth Market

Parts of Newcastle still follow the mediaeval street patterns with narrow roads and long thin plots. Some of the place names have also been carried through the centuries, as in the Groat Market on the bottom edge of the photograph, although not the Cloth Market, in the centre of the photograph, which was originally known as the Flesh Market until its name was changed in 1829. The markets have been in Newcastle for at least 800 years and probably much longer. Nowadays the area is popular for its bars and restaurants.

Newcastle Castle

The castle was built by Henry II between 1168 and 1178 on the site of an earlier motte-and-bailey castle and the original Roman Fort. The Black Gate on the left in the main image was added by Henry III. Although largely ruinous by the end of the 16th century, the castle was refortified during the English Civil War and besieged in 1644 by a Scottish parliamentarian force under Lord Levens. After a siege of several months, and with the Royalists refusing to surrender, the town was taken by storm following the blowing up of mines under the town walls. Once the walls had fallen the battle was short but bloody, with much hand-to-hand street fighting particularly around the Bigg Market, until the surviving Royalists eventually capitulated.

After the civil war the castle was used as a prison and restorations were carried out at various intervals from the early 19th century onwards. Unfortunately the castle was bisected by the railway viaduct in 1849. Nowadays it is protected by a Grade-I listing.

Above: Grey Street

Grey Street follows the line of a river, the Lort Burn, which was covered over in the 17th century. In the 19th century the area was developed by John Dobson and Richard Grainger, who produced the wonderful neoclassical architecture we see today.

Left: Amen Corner and Side

Newcastle is full of interesting street names: 'Amen Corner' is the official street name for the area adjacent the cathedral, and the road running down the side of the castle is called simply 'Side'. The area is noted for its Victorian architecture, restaurants and bars.

Above: The Metro Radio Arena
Opened in 1995, it has a capacity of 11,000. The arena has been used to stage a variety of sporting and music events and is the home of both Newcastle Vipers Ice Hockey team and Newcastle Eagles Basketball team.

Left: St Andrew's Church
Originally built in the 12th century, it has been much modified over the years, particularly after the civil war which left the building badly damaged. On the left of the image is the Chinese arch and just visible are the remains of the city walls which were undermined in the siege of 1644.

Above: The Royal Victoria Infirmary
The Royal Victoria Infirmary was founded in 1751, originally at Forth Bank, and the current site was opened by King Edward VII on 11 July 1906. The hospital has one of the biggest maternity units in the UK, with over 5,700 babies being born here each year. The hospital is also known for its leading burns unit and its ophthalmology department, which is one of the UK's largest treatment providers for cataracts.

Right: Spillers Quay
Spillers Quay is on the River Tyne at the confluence with the Ouseburn. The Free Trade Inn can be seen at the top of the image and the Ouseburn Regeneration Centre is on the right.

Above: The River Tyne looking west with the suburb of Walker in the middle and Newcastle and Gateshead City centres in the background. Running along the river bank in the centre of the image is the Walker Riverside Park, which was created by replacing former industrial land with wild flower meadows and woodland.

Left: The Central Exchange Buildings
The Central Exchange Buildings were built around 1837 to a design by John Wardle as part of Richard Grainger's regeneration master plan. Following a fire the Central Arcade was added in the middle of the building in 1906 to a design by J. Oswald & Sons.

The River Tyne is still the focus of much industrial activity, particularly relating to the North Sea oil and gas industry. Here we see the Wellstream works, which supply flexible pipelines for offshore marine use that are loaded onto huge cable-laying vessels such as the 'Team Oman' shown here. Built in the Netherlands in 1999, the CVL Team Oman can carry over 1,500 cubic meters of cable in its giant deck carousel and has a fuel consumption of 10 tons per day.

The Earl Grey Monument

The monument was built in 1838 to commemorate Charles Grey, 2nd Earl Grey, for his passing of the Great Reform Act of 1832 while Prime Minister. The Great Reform Act greatly extended the franchise and allowed people in the big industrial cities to vote while merging some rural constituencies with extremely small electorates. The act still left a large proportion of the male population and all women without a vote.

The column, designed by John and Benjamin Green, is hollow with a spiral staircase to the door on the platform, seen in the view above. The statue was sculpted by Edward Hodges Baily, who also created Nelson's Statue in Trafalgar Square.

Previous page, above, right and overleaf: The Newcastle Green Festival
The festival takes place every year in Leazes Park in the centre of Newcastle and is run, as the organisers say, to 'promote positive solutions to environmental problems and raise awareness of green and ethical issues', which it achieves through a variety of environmental groups, displays, art and music.

   The festival is run on a voluntary basis and owes its origins to the Newcastle University Green Party, who held the first fair in the Students' Union in 1995. In 1997 the fair moved to Leazes Park where it has grown into the massive event we see in the photographs.

Above: Jesmond Park West
Here is Jesmond Park West with Jesmond Dene Park running across the top left corner of the image. The school in the centre of the photograph is Heaton Manor School, which was rebuilt in 2004.

Right: Benton View Park
The offices of the Department of Work and Pensions at Longbenton, responsible for administering the UK's pensions and National Insurance contributions.

Overleaf: Jesmond
Looking east with much of North and South Tyneside in the background and the Jesmond Dene Park running across the image.

Above: Newcastle College Rye Hill Campus
The largest college in the North East, it is one of only 19 colleges in the UK to have been awarded Beacon status. It offers a wide variety of courses from part-time vocational to degree level. The college was graded as 'Grade I – outstanding' in the 2008 OFSTED reports and has managed to achieve a 97% pass rate for its A-level courses, with many subjects having a 100% pass rate.

Left: The Earl Grey Memorial looking down Grey Street.

St. James' Park

Newcastle United was founded in 1892 with the merger of Newcastle East End FC and Newcastle West End FC. Football has been played at St James' Park since 1880 and it is the North East's oldest football stadium. With a capacity of over 52,000, it is the Premier League's third largest stadium and the UK's seventh largest. The tight constraints of the city-centre location have led to the unusual asymmetric architecture. The stadium is scheduled to be used for the Olympic Games in 2012.

Northumbria University Newcastle City Campus East

Previously the Newcastle Polytechnic, the university was formed with the amalgamation of the Municipal College of Commerce, Rutherford College of Technology and the College of Art & Industrial Design in 1969. It offers almost 500 courses from undergraduate to postgraduate. The City Campus East, pictured left, is a new £70m development opened in 2007 which houses the Schools of Design, Law and Business. The building was designed to be environmentally friendly, with features such as solar panels for water heating and rainwater harvesting to provide water for the toilets. The new bridge linking the east and west campuses can be seen above.

Overleaf: The Northumbria University Newcastle City Campus West.

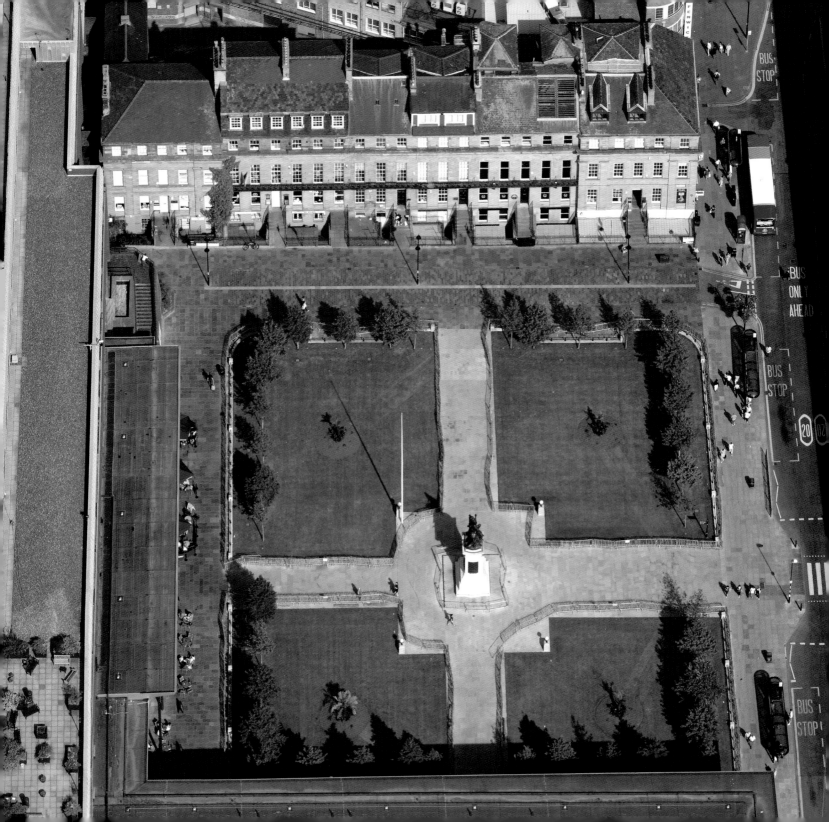

Above: Scrap metal recycling facility
If you have ever wondered what happens to scrap metal, here you can see how it is sorted before being shipped out to be melted down and made into new products.

Left: Old Eldon Square
In the centre of the square is a statue of St George and Dragon by Charles Leonard Hartwell constructed in 1923 as a memorial to the men lost in World War One. St George is the patron saint of the Northumberland Fusiliers. A copy of the statue was later erected in Marylebone, London. The square underwent a £1 million restoration in 2008 and was reopened with a VIP ceremony to rededicate the memorial.

Newcastle Central Station

Opened in 1850 by Queen Victoria and Prince Albert, the station was built to a design by John Dobson, in partnership with Robert Stephenson, for the Newcastle and Berwick Railway company. This became the North Eastern Railway in 1854 and then the London and North Eastern Railway in 1923. The three great curved roofs which dominate the image were the first of their type in the world and were expanded with the additional straight section at the end of the 19th century. The Newcastle Metro underground railway was added in 1981 and the main station building is Grade I listed.

Above: The Grade II listed Newcastle Civic Centre, home to Newcastle City Council, was opened in 1968 by the king of Norway and designed by city architect George Kenyon.

Right: St Nicholas Cathedral was first constructed soon after the Norman Conquest in the 11th century. The building was badly damaged by fire and restored in the 13th century, it was extended in the 14th century and had the tower added in the 15th century. The first moves to make the then parish church a cathedral were overturned by Queen Mary 1 (Bloody Mary) on her accession. The church finally became a cathedral in 1882 when Queen Victoria created the Diocese of Newcastle.

St Peter's Basin

All along the banks of the River Tyne the old industrial landscape is being regenerated and St Peter's Basin was one of the first to undergo this transformation, with its characterful quayside warehouses being turned into trendy new apartments and its dock providing moorings for yachts. The marina was the first city-centre marina in the North East and is also a Royal Yachting Association training centre.

Above: Clayton Street
Clayton Street in the city centre with St Mary's Cathedral in the foreground. St Mary's was built at a cost of £6,500 (£1 million in today's money) in 1844, to a design by Augustus Welby Northmore Pugin, and designated the Catholic Cathedral in 1850.

Left: Church of St Thomas the Martyr
The church is dedicated to Thomas Becket, Archbishop of Canterbury, who was murdered in 1170 by a group of knights wrongly believing they were carrying out the wishes of King Henry II. The current church is another masterpiece by local architect John Dobson, who designed much of Newcastle's classical architecture, and it was completed in 1830.

Gateshead

Above: The Tyne Bridges
The bridges connect Newcastle north bank on the left with Gateshead Quays on the right.

Right: The Gateshead Millennium Bridge
Designed by Wilkinson Eyre Architects and engineered by Gifford, the Gateshead Millennium Bridge is a unique tilting bridge. The £22 million structure provides a pedestrian and cycle link across the river and allows ships to pass as the whole structure pivots upwards, with the parabolic curve of the footway providing enough height for ships to clear underneath. The bridge won the 2002 RIBA Sterling prize.

Above: Tower blocks either side of the Gateshead Highway.

Previous page: The Angel of the North
Designed by Antony Gormley and erected in 1998, the Angel stands 66ft tall and 178ft from wing-tip to wing-tip, a wingspan which is around five times greater than my aircraft. Fabricated on Teesside by Hartlepool Steel Fabrications Ltd, the statue is the biggest in Britain and is anchored to the ground with more than 600 tons of concrete. Commissioned by Gateshead Council, the £1 million cost was funded by the National Lottery.

Above: In recent years Gateshead has seen a great deal of investment and new construction, such as this site at Quarryfield Road. This is not the first time the area has been rebuilt as the whole area was laid to waste in the great fire of Newcastle and Gateshead which broke out in Wilson & Sons worsted mill on Friday 6 October 1854. This spread to Bertram's warehouse, which contained sulphur and other combustible materials, causing a spectacular conflagration and drawing large crowds of onlookers. This resulted in many fatalities as the warehouse exploded in one of the largest detonations Britain had ever seen, which was heard more than 40 miles away.

Above: *The Tuxedo Princess* and the Tyne Bridge.

Left: The BALTIC Centre for Contemporary Art
The former Baltic Flour Mill was converted to the BALTIC Centre for Contemporary Art in 2002. The architect for the conversion was Dominic Williams of Ellis Williams Architects, who won the 1994 design competition for the project from the Royal Institute of British Architects (RIBA). The conversion involved gutting the original interior and constructing new floors to house the art display areas while at the same time preserving much of the original exterior. The rooftop houses a restaurant with panoramic views of Newcastle, Gateshead and the River Tyne.

Above: The Bowes Railway

Preserved as a museum, the railway was formerly a colliery railway constructed to take coal 15 miles down the line to the River Tyne at Jarrow. The oldest part of the railway was designed by George Stephenson. It opened in 1826 and now forms the preserved section. When it was in service the centre section of the line was steeply inclined and worked by rope haulage with locomotives used at each end of the line. The line was still in use in its entirety until 1968, with the last section becoming disused in 1974.

Left: Gateshead from the south east.

The banks of the River Tyne that once bustled with industrial activity are now being regenerated and are becoming desirable residential areas, such as the Staiths shown above. The site was originally a gasworks and coal yard and was later used for the Gateshead Garden Festival in 1990. The site is now being redeveloped by George Wimpey, with this new generation of designer homes being a dramatic break from the usual generic housing estate architecture.

A Class 142 Northern Rail DMU (Diesel Multiple Unit) commuter train, running towards Newcastle Central Station, approaches the King Edward VII Bridge. Tyneside is well-served with public transport, which is becoming increasingly important due to concerns about the environment and global warming.

Above: Allotments at Teams

It has been a centuries old tradition for families to grow their own fruit and vegetables, but it is a tradition that started to decline with the reductions in common land by the enclosure acts and the industrialisation of our towns and cities. The practice had declined so much that in 1908 the government passed the Small Holdings and Allotments Act to make adequate provision of land for families to rent.

Right: Boatyard at Felling Shore

Fishing is still an important industry in Tyneside with salmon nets present in the River Tyne, which is regarded by some as the best salmon river in England and Wales and is popular with anglers and commercial fishermen. As well as salmon, the river contains brown trout, sea trout, otters, crayfish, mussels, dace, chub, lamprey and eels.

Above: Flats on Mulgrave Terrace.

Right: Gateshead MetroCentre
Gateshead MetroCentre is Europe's largest shopping and leisure centre, containing nearly 330 shops and department stores and over 50 restaurants. It attracts more than 24 million visitors per year. Recent additions include the transport interchange, seen in the top left of the photograph, which connects the centre with the region's bus and rail network.

Previous page: The Gateshead International Stadium
The Gateshead International Stadium was opened in 1955 and is home to Gateshead Thunder Rugby League club, Gateshead FC and Gateshead Senators American Football team. The stadium also hosts athletics competitions.

The Gateshead Interchange

This opened in 1981 and provides surface connections to the bus network, including a MetroCentre shuttle and an underground station for the Tyne and Wear metro system. The metro system has 48 miles of track and carries out around 40 million journeys a year. It is one of only three underground systems in the UK, the others being London and Glasgow.

Bill Quay

A motor vehicle dismantler's yard at Bill Quay on the banks of the River Tyne. And it is not just the cars that are recycled, but also the yard itself, which is an old factory building. It is possibly one of the chemical works which dominated the Bill Quay area in the 19th century or one of the shipyard buildings, as building and refitting smaller ships was a major activity here in both the 19th and 20th centuries.

Ravensworth Castle

The two towers are the oldest remaining part of the castle and date from the 14th century, although it is likely that the castle's origins go back much further and it may even have been founded by the Saxons or Vikings. In the 18th century the castle was converted into a Gothic stately home to a design by Sir John Nash, who also designed Buckingham Palace. The owners of the castle, the Liddle family, derived much wealth from mining, but this was to be the castle's undoing as it was undermined by subsidence caused by the very mining activity that financed it. The last member of the family to reside here died in 1919, after which much of the grand furniture was sold off, and the building was used as a school before finally falling into ruin. The castle was featured in the BBC television programme *Restoration* but so far the extent of the subsidence and decay has made any restoration impossible.

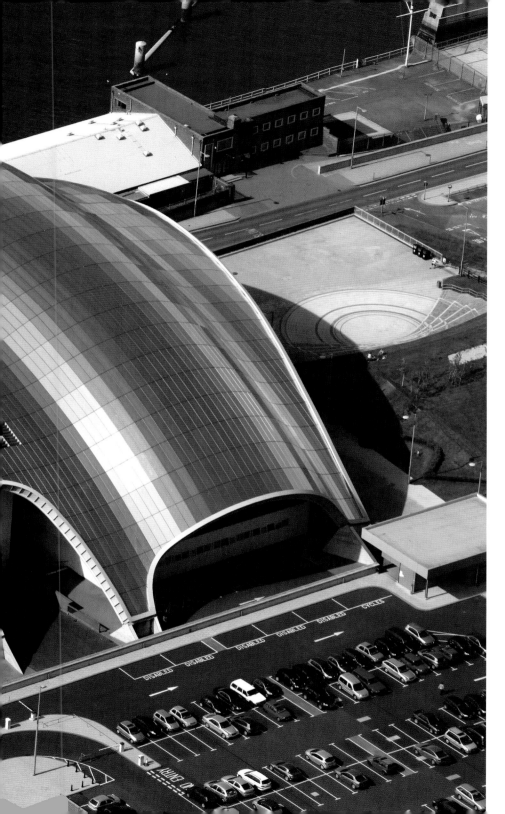

Left and overleaf: The Sage Building
Opened in 2004 and designed by Foster &
Partners for Gateshead Council, it is a
landmark structure that kick-started the
regeneration of the whole area. The
£70 million building was funded by the
National Lottery and houses two auditoria,
one with 1,700 seats and one with 400
seats, a rehearsal space and a 25-room
music education centre. It is renowned for
its outstanding acoustics and is home to the
Northern Sinfonia Orchestra. The building is
named after a sponsor – the Sage Group
PLC – a large software company.

Above: Trinity Square Shopping Centre

Trinity Square Shopping Centre was designed by Owen Luder in 1962 in the then popular brutalist style. The building was completed in 1969 and is shown here shortly before demolition in 2008. The building is most remembered for its appearance in the 1970 film *Get Carter*.

Right: St Mary's Church

The 900-year-old Grade I listed building is used as the Gateshead Visitors' Centre and hosts history and heritage displays. The building replaced an earlier church burned down by an angry mob in 1080 with the Bishop of Durham inside. The current building was badly damaged and narrowly missed complete destruction in the great fire of 1854 and was again damaged by fire in 1979, but it has since been restored.

Above: Saltwell Park

Saltwell Park was opened in 1876 and is the holder of many awards, including the Green Flag Award 2006 and the Civic Trust Park of the Year Award 2006. The park has recently undergone a £10 million restoration funded by the Heritage Lottery Fund and Gateshead Council. As can be seen in the photograph, the park is very popular and attracts more than two million visitors per year.

Right: Windmill Hills Town Park

Windmill Hills Town Park was Gateshead's first public park and takes its name from the numerous windmills that stood on the hill, which are commemorated by the wind vane sculpture seen in the centre of the image.

Above: Killingworth was built as a new town in the 1960s. The town is most famous for being the setting for the 1970s TV programme *Whatever happened to the likely lads.* The lake was constructed from a derelict pit and has recently been improved. The new leisure centre development at the top of the image is known as the Lakeside Centre and integrates indoor swimming pools with the waterside wildlife.

Right: St George's Church, Cullercoats, was built in 1884 to a design by J.L. Pearson. The Grade I listed Anglican church is famous for its organ made by T.C. Lewis.

Previous page: Cullercoats.

Above: The 'Big Kid Circus' visited Cullercoats and Tynemouth in the summer of 2008.

Right: The Cullercoats Lifeboat Station was opened after a boat taking a pilot out to a ship capsized and resulted in the loss of all seven men. This prompted the Duke of Northumberland to fund the station and a self-righting lifeboat was designed, which entered service in 1852. The current boathouse was constructed in 1896, and the watch house above it was built in 1879. The lifeboats were powered by oars and sail until the arrival of the first motorboat in 1937, which tragically overturned in 1939 and a number of lives were lost. Nowadays the station houses one of the fast inflatable lifeboats which have been a great success for the RNLI.

Overleaf: Cullercoats.

Smith's Dock, North Shields.

As the older, heavy industries have declined, the banks of the River Tyne have been transformed into desirable residential areas. These images show the former Smith's Docks and A&P ship repair yard in 2008, part way through the transformation, as some of the dry docks are filled in and the ground is prepared for the construction of some 1,200 homes. Designed by a 14-strong team of architects, the scheme will include houses, apartments, shops and cafés. The centrepiece will be 'The Bullring', a pair of apartment blocks built on the large, dry docks, leaving the centre dock as a water feature between them.

The Fish Quay

The quay is a vibrant hub of activity, not just for the fishing industry but also for diverse businesses from electronics to artists' studios. The settlement can trace its roots back to the 13th century, when it grew up serving Tynemouth Monastery. On the right of the lighthouse in the shot above is Clifford's Fort, which was built in 1672 to protect the quay from Dutch warships. Also in the image are the two white towers called the Highlights and the Lowlights. Built in 1808, they are used by ships to align themselves with the river and harbour entrance. In the days of shipping, the bend in the River Tyne, seen here on the left, was known as Comedy Corner as it was easy to make a mistake navigating a large sailing ship round such a sharp bend.

Above: *The Earl of Zetland* at Royal Quays Marina in North Shields. Built at Aberdeen in 1939, the ship was formerly a cargo and passenger ferry serving the Shetland Isles until 1973. After a short period in oil company service under the name of *Celtic Surveyor*, she is now used as a floating restaurant. The marina has been built in the old Albert Edward Dock and is now one of the North East's top marinas.

Right: *The Princess of Norway,* which was built in 1986 by Schichau Seebeckwerft AG in Bremerhaven. The 31,356 ton DFDS ferry can carry 1,290 passengers and 550 cars. She currently serves on the route from North Shields to Ljmuiden in Holland.

Above: A cricket match being played at the Prior's Park, Tynemouth.

Right: Front Street in Tynemouth, popular for its pubs, hotels and boutiques.

Overleaf: Tynemouth Priory, founded by Edwin of Northumbria in the seventh century. It was an important destination for pilgrims visiting the grave of St Oswain. The monks attempted to fortify the site, but it was repeatedly attacked by the Danes throughout the ninth century. Stone walls were built around the priory in 1296 and a gatehouse was constructed in 1300. The monastery was disbanded and largely dismantled in 1538 during Henry VIII's Reformation, although the church remained in use until 1668. A lighthouse stood on the site from 1775 to 1895, and from the 19th century through both world wars the site was used as an artillery battery. The modern building on the left was the coastguard building until its closure in 2001.

Above: A close up of one of the artillery batteries at Tynemouth Priory. Originally constructed in 1902 to house a breach loading gun, the gun battery was in service throughout World War One and Two and was updated with 6-inch naval guns, one of which is now preserved on its original mount.

Right: The remains of the 12th-century Priory Church still almost reach their original height. Although the Priory was dissolved by Henry VIII, the church remained in use until a new church was built elsewhere in 1668.

Above: Percy Gardens, Tynemouth. This neat Victorian crescent has an unusual feature: the white tower on the right was originally the fire control tower for the nearby gun batteries. Built during World War Two, the tower has now been converted into a unique dwelling.

Left: The monument to Admiral Lord Collingwood, whose ship, *The Royal Sovereign*, fired the first shot at the Battle of Trafalgar, was constructed in 1845. Collingwood's role in the battle was crucial, as he eventually took command of the British fleet when Nelson was shot, leading them to victory. If Collingwood had lost, Britain would have been invaded by Napoleon, whose army was poised ready across the English Channel. The monument was designed by John Dobson, and the Portland stone sculpture was created by John Graham Lough. The canon are from *The Royal Sovereign*, and are the only surviving canon from the Battle of Trafalgar outside HMS *Victory*.

Left: Long Sands Beach busy with tourists enjoying a summer evening by the sea. The beach is very popular with large numbers of visitors from nearby Newcastle, who come to swim, surf or just sunbathe on the golden sand. The British Surfing Championships were held here in 2003, and the beach holds a Blue Flag award, which means it has met 29 criteria for water quality, environmental education, environmental management, safety and services.

Above, left and overleaf: The former Swan Hunters Shipyard at Wallsend, shown here in 2008 during dismantling, with the equipment being prepared for shipment to an Indian shipyard. Started in 1880, Swan Hunter was Britain's most famous shipbuilder. The firm is still in business but nowadays designs ships rather than builds them. Ships constructed here include the RMS *Mauritania*, RMS *Carpathia,* which went to the aid of the *Titanic*, the *Atlantic Conveyor* of Falklands War fame, the MV *Derbyshire*, the current HMS *Ark Royal* and HMS *Edinburgh,* from the wreck of which four and a half tons of gold were recovered in the Barents Sea. The last ship built here was the RFA *Lyme Bay,* which ran late and over budget and sealed the yard's fate.

Previous page: Swan Hunters and the Tyne taken at the time of closure in November 2006 .

Above: The Dome, Spanish City, Whitley Bay, opened in 1910 as a permanent fairground. The Grade II listed building is currently being restored as part of a wide ranging £60 million regeneration of the whole area, which will include new homes, offices and hotels. Once a ballroom, the Dome will soon re-emerge as a visual and performing arts centre.

Left: 'The Gut', home of Willington Quay Boat Club. Pleasure boats have been thriving on the Tyne in recent years, although things are expected to dampen down with a sudden dramatic increase in the tax on boat fuel in 2008.

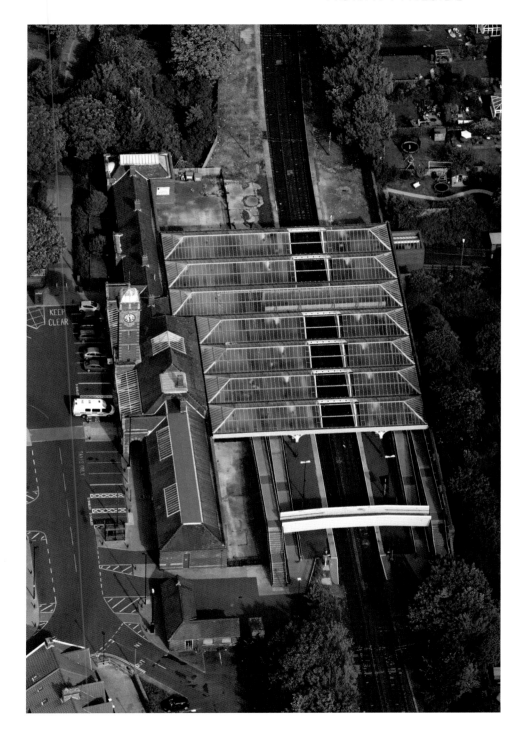

Previous page: Whitley Bay

Far left: Static caravans at Whitley Bay.

Left: Whitley Bay Metro Station was originally constructed in 1910 for the North Eastern Railway Company. The Grade II listed station now forms part of the Metro System.

Overleaf: St Mary's Lighthouse. Opened in 1898 to replace an older lighthouse that stood on Tynemouth Priory, it was intended that the new lighthouse would be more visible positioned away from the smoke of the shipping in the Tyne. Despite the lighthouse some ships were still lost, notably the Barque *California* in 1913, the remains of which can still be seen at low tide. The cottage was built in 1855 as a fisherman's cottage, although for a time it was used as a pub.

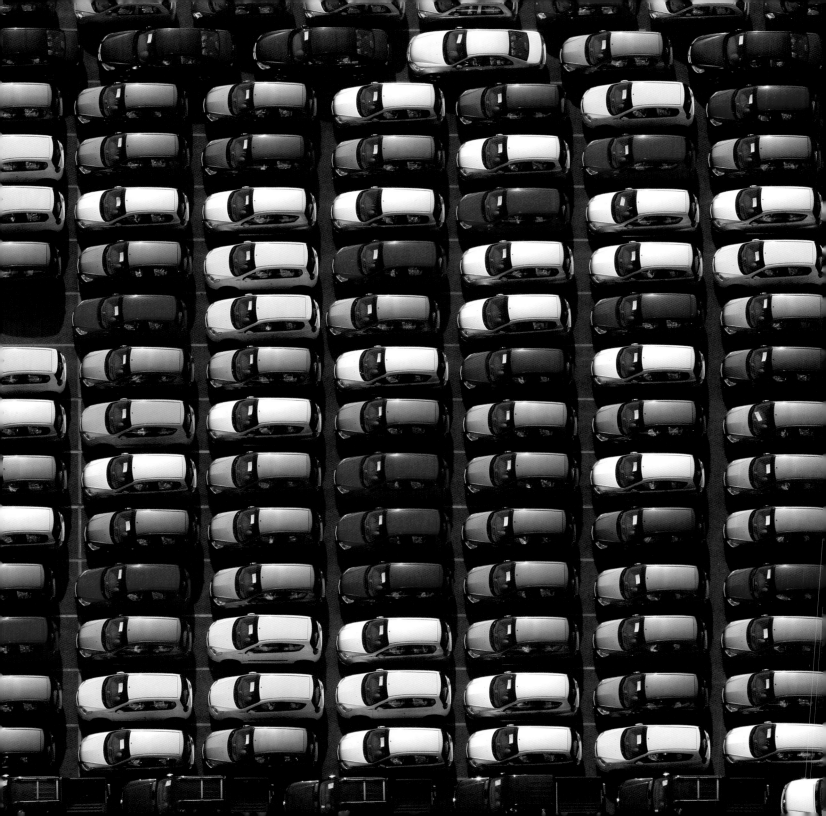

South Tyneside

Above: Golfers playing at Whitburn Golf Club. Opened in 1934, the course is known for its sea views

Previous page: New cars, mainly Chevrolet Aveos, waiting on the quayside at the Port of Tyne car terminal in South Shields. Reflecting the multinational nature of business, the cars wear an American badge but were actually built in Warsaw. There has been a port here since Roman times, when it was used to supply the forts along Hadrian's Wall. The port boomed during the Industrial Revolution with the export of coal, but in a strange twist of fate the port is now used to import coal.

Hebburn Eco Centre was built in 1996 using sustainable construction techniques and materials, including recycled bricks and a roof made from recycled drinks cans. Power is provided by the wind turbine, backed up by solar cells. The centre provides office space for small businesses and the Groundwork Trust, which promotes employment and regeneration through environmentally friendly means.

The A & P shipyard at Hebburn specialises in converting ships, and in the image above the ice-breaking cargo ship *Ice Maiden I* is being converted into a harsh weather accommodation ship or 'flotel' to house up to 400 people. The drydock, at 45×259m, is one of the largest in Northern England. There are plans to construct a giant 120m-tall wind turbine at the site, which will be one of the largest structures ever built on the Tyne. The turbine will provide power for the yard's planned ship recycling scheme.

Above: The *Svitzer Maltby* Marine Tug, built in 2005 in Lithuania. She is registered in Middlesbrough.

Right: The Northern Producer is seen here being refurbished at the McNulty facility at Tyne Dock, South Shields. The vessel is a semi-submersible, floating production installation used in the North Sea with a capacity of 55,000 barrels of oil per day. She was originally built as a drilling rig and was then converted to a floating production facility in 1991. Following this refurbishment, she has been stationed 150km off the coast of the Shetland Islands to serve the Don South-West and West Don Oil Fields, where oil is extracted from a depth of 11,000ft.

The South Shields ferry terminal, with the ferry *Shieldsman* closest and the *Pride of the Tyne* behind. There has been a ferry service connecting North and South Shields since the 14th century, with the passengers currently crossing for a pound. The *Shieldsman* was built in Pembroke Dock in 1976 by Hancock Shipbuilders and is now retired from service, having been replaced by the *Spirit of the Tyne* which entered service in 2007. She was constructed at Harlingen in the Netherlands and then fitted out at the Halmatic yard in Portsmouth at a total cost of £1.9million.

Above: The Tyne Pilot boat *Norman Forster* speeds past the Groyne and Bell Tower at South Shields. The marine pilot is a local expert navigator who has the important task of guiding ships through the dangerous river mouth and into or out of the ports. The Port of Tyne has three pilot boats which can be seen working in all weathers.

Overleaf: The Thompson Celebration Cruise Ship leaves the River Tyne and heads out into the North Sea.

Above: Market Dock, South Shields.
One of many docks converted to residential use, it is noted for its seven stainless steel sculptures of sailing ships laid out in what used to be Brigham and Cowans dry dock. Previously the dock was used for ship repair, and Mulberry Harbour sections were constructed here during the war.

Left: Marsden Rock, South Shields.
As the sea has eroded the cliffs, it has left behind this limestone stack which provides an ideal home for Kittiwakes, Cormorants and Fulmars. The rock used to be significantly larger, but a partial collapse in 1996 left a smaller second stack which had to be demolished with explosives for safety reasons.

Above: The Customs House, South Shields. Dating from 1848, the building is now used as an arts centre, hosting dance, film, theatre and visual art.

Right and overleaf: The Souter Lighthouse, Whitburn, was the world's first electric lighthouse. Opened in 1871 and in use until 1988, the building is now maintained by the National Trust. The structure in the foreground is the foghorn station, which was said to be the loudest in the UK and could be heard from Sunderland to Whitley Bay.

photo: Ian Hay / Flight Images

The Arbeia Roman Fort, South Shields, was built around AD 160 on the site of an Iron Age settlement to guard the entrance to the River Tyne. It was called Arbeia because it was originally garrisoned by Arabs from the Tigris area. Around AD 200 it was redeveloped with additional granaries to provide a supply base for Hadrian's Wall, which ended just up the river at Wallsend. Around AD 300 the fort was burnt down, but it is not clear if that was due to military action. It was rebuilt but finally abandoned when the Romans left Britain in AD 410. The West Gate was reconstructed in 1986 over the original remains, followed by the Commanding Officer's house in 2002.